LITTLE SARAH

The birth, life works, and motherhood
of LITTLE SARAH

SARAH COBB

authorHOUSE

AuthorHouse™
1663 Liberty Drive
Bloomington, IN 47403
www.authorhouse.com
Phone: 833-262-8899

Published by AuthorHouse 05/24/2021

ISBN: 978-1-6655-2548-0 (sc)
ISBN: 978-1-6655-2547-3 (e)

A motivational Autobiography of a Southern Country Girl

(Cotton Stalks)　　　　　　　　(Cotton Field)

From Cotton field poverty To Blessings, Blessings and more Blessings.

Teaching at Sunday School

A Christian / Motivational Autobiography

An autobiographical life story with family, characters, about a child who grew up in small Southern towns and eventually migrated North to complete her education.

Characters: The black Cobb offspring from Master Cobb's plantation.

1. Head of Household: Arthur L. Cobb, Sr.
2. Mother: Etha Mae Coleman-Cobb

   Siblings:

   1. Willie J. Cobb - Deceased
   2. Willie L. Cobb – Deceased
   3. Silas Cobb, Sr. – Deceased
   4. Theodore Cobb – Deceased
   5. Robert L. Cobb – Deceased
   6. Arthur L. Cobb, Jr.
   7. Dorothy J. Cobb
   8. Sarah M. Cobb
   9. Ellis Cobb by Arthur's 3rd wife last egg swimming – deceased 2016
   10. 1 – deceased at birth (female)
   11. 1 – deceased at birth (male)
   12. Leotis Butts-Cobb – stepsister

3. Paternal Grandparents:
   Johnny L. Cobb, Sr. (Deep red complexion)
   Minnie L. Cobb (Dark complexion)

I never knew my mother's parents, except a step-grandfather named Tobe Grayer. Maternal step-grandfather Grayer had a wagon and a mule. I only remember riding in the wagon once with him and as I grew up, he passed away. I don't recall how old I was, but I do remember this onetime event.

CONTENTS

DEDICATION

This next book is being dedicated to my parents: Arthur Lee Cobb, Sr. and Etha Mae Cobb.

First, to *my heavenly father, my Lord and Savior Jesus Christ*, I loved my parents. Now that I am a parent and Grandparent the order changes to my heavenly father, my Lord and Savor Jesus Christ; My daughter (God's child) Heather Shantelle Cobb, and her 13-year-old son (Definitely God's child) Jordon Ronell Jones; maybe later his name may change to Jordon Ronell Jones-Cobb.

To paraphrase a scripture from the KJV bible "The road to salvation is narrow, but the road to destruction is wide." I equate this with big churches being the wide road and the small family-like churches being the narrow road.

My church family-The original St. James Missionary Baptist Church and "The Church of God." At the time of this writing, we are approximate 10 in membership, a close-knit family under the Christian teaching of Dr. Karl Reid whose famous quote in my opinion is "Y'all getting anything out of this?" We are in a store front on the lower Eastside of Detroit, Michigan.

I especially dedicate this novel to: My prayer partner, my sister in

Christ, and my friend. The church administrator is whom I speak of; without her help and her spiritual soul, I could not have written this "Help Book."

Also, to my adopted son, Bryan Jones, for without his technological skills and the time he has devoted to assisting me getting it ready to go to press, I definitely could not have accomplished this. Thank you, Bryan. God Bless and keep you in your life ventures – much success is with you!!

ACKNOWLEDGMENTS

The most high God is my first acknowledgment because without the miracle he bestowed upon me, I would not be here telling my life experiences.

My mother, Etha Mae Coleman, deceased at my birth is my next acknowledgement. Although I never knew you, I love you with all my heart.

Finally, all of the positive and negative experiences I encountered during my life span; experiences that I've learned from and was able to grow stronger in my spiritual journey. In this acknowledgment, experience equals the people who became part of my life for short and long periods. In writing this I pray that some individual can read it and learn that *hope is always in your favor as long as you believe!*

PROLOGUE

This is a collection of my life story which entails birth combined with death, the daunting trial of the wash kettle leading to the Cripple Children Association (now United Foundation), and Grady's Memorial Hospital.

I will also share my nuclear family, no, not that it was explosive, but how we became the Cobb family, with an older sister who was an authoritarian, sibling ships and step siblings, a new meaning to stepmothers and how being the youngest child meant I was always learning and listening to my siblings to know what was going on and what had brought us to this point in our family history. And let's find out if doing your chores can actually lead to a whipping (porch scrubbing). The place was Home, Hospital, School and Cotton Fields. There would be other fields as well, but I will leave you with that.

Sometimes running away from a problem can enable you to do what you really should be doing (finish school), living away from home, my oldest brother and his wife, high school, friends, and even suicidal thoughts. It was tough growing up without a mother in poverty as it was known. Yet, I found a way to get beyond high school and to even migrate North.

I landed in Detroit, Michigan in 1971 and that is where I bring you this story from today. *I pray that you will enjoy this autobiography, which is really my testimony of overcoming, loving, praying and praising.*

This is the story of Little Sarah.

INTRODUCTION

When I was very young, age 12, 13, I used to love to read romance books, I enjoyed love stories, and happy endings. I think it had a lot to do with the way my life was going at the time. My Dad was on his second marriage and I was in and out of Grady's hospital in Atlanta, Georgia. It was summertime in Cordele, Georgia. The blackberries and plums were all ready for the picking.

My father was a sharecropper and farm hand supervisor. Cotton, watermelon, peanuts, peaches, okra, and tobacco were all ripe for the season. My father's truck rolled out each morning between 5:00-6:00 am. From 6:00 am to 6:00 pm we did whatever the crop was for the day.

About 6:00 pm the end of the workday comes with gladness. Home was dinner, bath, and bed. If cotton was the crop of the day and our then stepmother (#4), who was mean, obsessed, illiterate and angry, felt we didn't pick enough cotton, she found chores around the house for us to do. My dad would escape across the street to Uncle Johnny's house.

One day my sister decided that she was no longer going to take the beatings that happened when stepmother thought we didn't pick enough cotton for the day. Sister ran over to Uncle Johnny's to tell daddy that stepmother was going to whip us. Daddy came to our rescue, ordered us to bath and bed. Stepmother was angry.

This was the time we decided to run away to live with our older brother and his wife, who had no children. Little did we know we were jumping out of the "frying pan and into the fire." We executed our plan by lying about not getting promoted unless we come to school the last day.
Our last day was sad, because I loved my dad and didn't want to leave him, but I didn't leave without leaving him a letter of all the physical abuse we suffered without his knowledge.

Stepmother was angry that we were allowed to go to school that last day because she was illiterate and only wanted us to work. Daddy wanted his girls to be educated, so we won our last day.

We had planned for our brother to pick us up after school. Our plan went well, we were able to leave and say goodbye to our angry, new stepmother.

Our new life will be discussed in the body of this book.

Religion was important to my dad and us. We were baptized at the age of 12 in a muddy creek at the Gum Creek Baptist Church. *God was forever with us. I thank God each day for keeping us in his care. As we matured in our lives, we learned the true goodness of God and how he carried us through our young lives and on to adult lives. God is good all the time, and all the time God is good.*

Chapter One

HOW IT ALL BEGAN

1947 was a hard time for most poor black families. The war had just ended, and labor was short in demand. It was a very good year; May 3rd was excellent. On a warm, southern day, deep in the country woods of Cordele, Georgia a precious little baby girl was being born. On this warm summer day in Georgia, the flowers were in full bloom and the wind was warm. This would be the tenth child born to Etha and Arthur Cobb. Mid-wives were the norm for poor blacks in this small southern, racist town. Hospital births were only for the whites. I was the 10th child born of a mother, who was only 38 years old at the time of my birth and her death. Married to a sharecropper who, after a long day of work, found comfort in sexual activities with his wife.

<u>Father</u>

My father, Arthur Lee, was a labor boss who took people to the fields to do labor, he was paid by the number of people he brought to the fields. My siblings were four of those laborers. Eight males and two females made up the family of Arthur Lee and Etha Mae Cobb. We would work from 6am until 6pm in the fields for $3.00 per pound of cotton. My father had a physical handicap with his left arm, therefore physical work for him was impossible. You see, my dad was handicapped, one of his hands was bent and he could not use it. I am sure now, that he had some kind of stroke, or maybe he was born that way. Field supervisor was all he could be. This meant he was responsible for getting the field hands to the field to get the work done for the farm owner. Pay for him was .50 cents a head for each person he brought and any other perk he would receive from the farm owner.

Being the youngest of ten children in the family I had little knowledge of what went on. My life began after my birth at home I assume. I now know that shortly after my birth my mother passed away. So, 1947 was also the year my mother's spirit went to heaven. As an adult I've been able to put pieces together surrounding her death, the cause and how it happened.

Uncle Bud

My favorite uncle said one time in one of his drunken stupors that "I killed (my) mother." I suppose he meant that after my birth she never recovered. My uncle, her brother, Foster Ingram, was my favorite uncle. "Uncle Bud" as he was affectionately called by members of the family, was illiterate and a functional alcoholic. My uncle married a functional alcoholic single mom, who became my aunt Thelma. Aunt Thelma was a sophisticated alcoholic single mom; my uncle married her, raised her then beautiful daughter Evelyn and took very good care of both of them.

Although she was who she was, she felt that she and her daughter were better than other people. Aunt Thelma always referred to us as, "These are Foster's nieces" when introducing us to others. Evelyn was put on a pedestal by her mother, and a lot of regular children she was not allowed to associate with. My Aunt Thelma became diabetic and had to have insulin shots. Her daughter Evelyn came over to the house and fixed five insulin needles for her mother to take. That was her way of taking care of her mother. Prior to Aunt Thelma's death, her daughter Evelyn went into her bank account and took out all of her saved social security to open up a flower shop on East Warren and Conner in Detroit. Shortly after, my aunt passed away. I think she was so heartbroken that she had no will to live.

In the early years as poor children in Georgia, my uncle Bud and his family came to Georgia in the middle of the morning with boxes of clothes for my sister and I. What joy this brought to our lives! Being poor, our clothing was very minimal. Our wardrobe consisted of 2 pair of shoes and a lot of homemade dresses. One pair of shoes was black patent leather shoes for church, the other a pair of black and white moccasin with a very thick sole. Their lifetime was one year; how I use to try to cut some of the thick sole away, to get a pair of penny loafers like other kids. This never happened.

The woman my father was seeing while still married to my mother moved in after my mother died. At this time in the Cobb household, Daddy was with the woman whom I came to know as my real mom, Lessie Mae Sherman. My oldest brothers had left home to find their way in life. Arthur Lee, Sr. taught them strong work ethics, marriage, woman and family. Although they had minimal to no formal education, they were able to survive. The last four siblings were left at home at this time. The last four siblings were each approximate 1-2 years apart in age: Robert Lee, being the oldest, Arthur Lee, Jr. the second oldest, then Dorothy Jean, and Little Sarah the baby.

Years later knowing that she was dying, she felt the need to tell me she felt obligated to help my father raise his ten kids. I don't recall how I found out she was not my real mother.

Her confession also let me know what happened to me as a baby. It turns out I had crawled and gotten some potash (poison) and swallowed it while I was supposed to be watched by one of my older brothers.

Mama Lessie shared during her surprising confession that in those days southern people often washed clothes outside in a black kettle heated by wood fire. Wood fires help to get the clothes clean. Also used was a poison substance called (potash) lye, a white crystal substance added to the clothes in the kettle to aid in their cleaning.

"I talk so much" as a result of what happened next in my childhood. This story was told to me by my 1st stepmom (Lessie Mae) when I was 31 years old. I was a mother by then with a 2-year-old daughter living in Detroit, Michigan.

According to Mama Lessie, she was outside washing one day. After using the lye, she partially put the top back on it. I was in crawling stages and my 2 years older brother Arthur and Robert were supposed to be watching me. Later I would learn that one would blame the other for what happened next. On this day of washing, I was crawling around the yard, supposedly being watched by my brothers. My mom had not closed the top on the container of lye securely. At this stage everything babies saw, the first place was to put it in their mouth. I was told I tipped over the can and put some of the poison in my mouth to eat. What happen next took (14) fourteen years to correct.

By putting potash in my mouth and swallowing even a small amount caused traumatic damage. My mouth was drawn so tight, only the size of a small pea was left open. Cripple Children Organization became a necessary part of my life. This organization helped poor people get medical help for serious medical conditions because their parents could not afford to pay for medical service. Cripple Children organization later become The United Way Organization. During my years of employment, I always gave to the United Way fund as a way of giving back. Upon my departure from this earth, instead of flowers I will request that funds be given or made to the UFD in my memory.

After the Lye incident, years of surgery and trips to Atlanta, Georgia became my lifestyle for the next 14 years. I would learn later that a lot of hospital staff became attached to me, and because my dad and family lived far from Atlanta and was not able to visit, some of the Caucasian nurses would take me home with them for weekends. I recall watching the other children get visits and some of their family would smile at me. When other families came to visit at the hospital, I was the child who got no visits, so they often brought me coloring books and toys.

As I became school age; the visits would always interrupt my school time. When it was time to go back to Atlanta for another operation, I would get a post card with date and time to be there. I dreaded the interruption in my school and being away from my family, but it was necessary. My mom and I would catch the train or bus and make the trip. Mom couldn't stay, so I was alone again with Grady's Memorial staff.

The Lye bruised my lips, my throat, my vocal cords and my right lung. As a child in school because the lye affected my vocal cords, my voice never developed past my baby voice, so I got a lot of teasing because of my burned lips and my baby-like voice. After years of not being able to talk while they literally reopened my mouth is "why I now talk so much." I suppose I am trying to catch up, having 14 years to make up. I endured the teasing from my peers because there was nothing I could do about it.

Each time it was time to go home my mother would come and get me. Oh, how I looked forward to the train rides and the time alone with my mother. I loved my mom so very much, and I believed she loved me.

My father was always busy working and my 2 brothers, and my older sister were working as well. I guess my dad had to work and Atlanta was a long way away.

Because I was sickly and the baby, while my mother was there, I never had to work. My sister was very bossy like my father's sister (Aunt Annie Bell). I guess she felt she was looking after me because she was older and could tell me what to do. We often got into sisterly squabbles because I resented her being bossy with me as if she was my mother.

At age 14, my father and mommy, Lessie Mae Sherman, and I made my final trip to Atlanta, Grady's Memorial Hospital, where I had the last of my numerous operations. This last trip to Atlanta, Grady's Memorial Hospital was to set the tone for the rest of my life. In the south, the tradition was, when grown-ups got together, children were nowhere around except they slipped or hid so they could hear what was being said. All I was told was that I was to have a serious operation. I recall two doctors standing over my bed saying to each other, "If she makes it through this, she will be alright." This had to be a serious operation because I was flat on my back for a long time, with my chest bandaged up. Later I would learn that they removed part of my right lung.

Prior to the operation I recall walking around the children's ward where I was, and seeing other family members with their children, remembering that I was far from home and no one would be with me as other family members were with their children. I remember feeling very sad because I felt so alone without my family.

In 1960 I am not sure whether modern technology had invented a shot of sleep medicine (anesthesia) to put you to sleep prior to your operation or not. My family being poor and having to have free medical service through the Cripple Children Organization, I am sure they used the least expensive sleep medicine they had.

From the time of my first surgery to open my mouth, I had many, many operations. I recall once I was old enough to know what was going on, I remember an instrument that resembled a sifter (a tool used to separate lumps from flour) and a cloth being put over my nose and the nurse talking to me, telling me to count from 1-10. The liquid anesthesia then was called ether (pronounced in the south like "etha"), the smell was horrible, but it was very strong. I don't think I ever made it to number ten in counting because of the strength of etha. I will never forget that smell. Thank God, they later began using the shot.

At this point a long period of recovery began, most of the time I had to remain flat on my back. As days went on, the nurses and doctors would come, change bandages and tell me about the progress I was making and what the operation included.

As I recovered, I remembered sitting by the elevator one day watching other families come to visit their children praying my family would come. Suddenly the elevator door opened and out stepped my dad, my aunt and my oldest brother. My heart was filled with so much joy. This was my first visit from my family ever.

My joy would soon turn to sorrow because when it was time for me to go home, my mother didn't come for me. It was my aunt. I knew something was wrong. As children then you didn't ask grownups questions. As we started the train ride home, I started to get sick. By the time we got home I was weak and sick. I saw this big truck in front of our house. Then I began to ask, "Where is my mother?" No answer was given, and I was taken straight to bed. The house was disarranged as if someone was moving. I really became worried.

Finally, my mother came to my bed side. Her words I still remember, "Baby, your mother has to leave, and your daddy won't let me take you with me" I asked "Why?" but was given no answer. Her next words were if I try to see you, he will have me put in jail. My mother said she would meet me at school one day next week. My heart was so broken. I didn't understand what was going on, all I knew was I was losing my mother. The following days were a mere nightmare. Every day at school I went to the side of the building where she said she would meet me. Day after day, I couldn't wait for recess to come so I could rush to our meeting place. After about a week, one day she showed up. I was overjoyed to see her, but only to learn that she was leaving town. My Aunt Queen, who lived across the street and was blind, would be our contact person.

I wrote letters for my Aunt Queen to her daughter. Mother said she would write me at my aunt's house, and when I came over to her house, I could read my letter and write her back. My dad was never to know this. My mom gave me 10 dimes for me and 10 for my sister, and then she was gone. Coming home from Grady's, realizing now my mom was gone, my life would never be the same. I felt so alone. I remember sitting on the porch one day, thinking how lonely it is without my mother.

Cordele and Americus, Georgia

The traffic that ran down Highway 41 was busy. We lived in a place down Highway 41 from the projects and the rest of the town. Cordele, Georgia was a small southern town, much like Americus, Georgia, being only 32 miles apart with a bridge that covered Flint River for miles and miles. For years, the pathway across Flint River was only 2 lanes wide, or narrow, if you really want the truth. It was very frightening to drive across it for fear that you may drive over the side.

Our area of Cordele was called New-town. Below New-Town was a

Georgia state prison. As a child I recalled sitting on the porch and watching the prisoners on the chain gang build Highway 41.

The ditch across from 2908 Turner Street where we were living was full of blackberries. One day my cousin, Betty and I were picking blackberries and we started running from dogs and the faster we ran, the faster the dogs ran. As we stopped running in the blackberry bushes the dogs stopped running. This day I learned an important lesson. "Never run from dogs, because as you run, the dogs run; when you stop running, they stop." I still have marks on my legs where the blackberry bushes sticky spurs caused sores on my legs.

One day while picking blackberries in the ditch I got bitten on my foot by a snake. My foot had to be treated and bandaged for a long period of time. The snake bit me between my big toe and the one next to it. Each day I had to sit on the porch with my foot elevated until it healed.

With Mama gone would be the beginning of a different life for me and my three (3) siblings. Our home was a six-room house with 2 boys and 2 girls. We kept it clean, cooked and we took care of each other.

The two boys had the biggest case of sibling rivalry you can ever imagine. Their rivalry often ended in physical encounters as young boys that had to be stopped by my father, who was truly head of his household, always. They loved each other dearly, and whatever one had, the other one had to have something like it or better. Sibling rivalry between my two younger brothers had escalated by this time to being physical. My father's discipline was to get a big stick himself and make them fight until they passed out.

Little did we know or understand that our father was not about to be without a wife. Shortly after Mama Lessie departed my dad began his line of marriages. The next thing we knew was our father came home with 8 children on the back of his truck and a new wife. Now we had 12 children and 2 adults in a six-room house. Life was not easy but, we had nothing to say about it. In those days adults didn't consult children about anything, they made the decisions and the children accepted it.

My two younger brothers fought with their stepbrothers and my sister and I tried to get along with our stepsisters. Our house stayed a mess and mealtime was always a rush. If you were late, you got what was left to eat. This went on and on. I don't remember my stepmother being pregnant because she was a big-framed woman. I do remember when she brought my little brother home from the hospital. It was winter and we children sat around the fireplace, as she gave my dad the most wonderful news we could ever hear. Their marriage was over, and she and her 9 children were leaving.

Something about her children and his children were not getting along. All I remember is thinking we can now have our home back. I think she and my father had a messy divorce and she tried to take whatever my dad had. My aunt, Annie Bell, who was my dad's older sister, must have come to my dad's rescue, as she always did. I think she was acting as his protector. We didn't see our stepsiblings much after that, not even our little baby brother. We heard that they lived in the projects somewhere We cleaned our house and things appeared to be back to normal. However, we were in for a big surprise.

Our father's next wife would give a new meaning to the word "stepmom." Again, without any notice, up came another wife with her big boobs, and green cat eyes. I think she gave my dad six hundred dollars as she moved in. We would later find this out from the many fights and arguments they were to have.

This wife was my first knowledge of an illiterate person. My dad taught her to count, and I am not sure to this day if she could read. This stepmom was a good cook, this I know, although she appeared to have no experience in being a mother. My two older brothers decided early on that she was not going to be their stepmother. Arthur Jr. left first, to go to Americus, Georgia to live with our oldest brother and his wife who had no children. Robert left after one night when the stepmom tried to whip him and he fought back. I remember my dad getting the broom stick as Robert and his stepmom tussled and eggs were broken that she had in her arms. Robert left to join his brother in Americus. These two were very close, although as boys they fought each other a lot. As I now recall my 6 other brothers had long left home and lived in other parts of Georgia. I also later learned that I had a stepsister, Leotis.

My stepmother was a very mean-spirited person. She made me get off my daddy's lap and sit on the floor. I believe because she was not educated, she didn't want my sister and me to be. All she wanted us to do was go to the fields and work. Most of the time we had to lie to our dad so that we could go to school. When we had to work the fields, we couldn't talk to our cousins as we worked. If she caught us talking, we would look up and like a big thunderstorm, she would make her way over and whip us right on the spot with a cotton stalk. Rumor was that she had a son, who joined the army and never came back; believe me I could understand why.

Prior to this, his 4th marriage, I had never heard my dad argue or use profanity. This marriage was full of violent fights and our stepmother could swear like a sailor. My sister and I were very frightened when their fights and arguments would start at the front of the house and end up in the back of it. The neighbors felt sorry for us but never got involved. Each time we would hear her say, "Give me my money and I will go." We used to pray that daddy would just give her her money so she could go. When we did manage to go to school, it would make her angry. She would find things to whip us about and she would leave a long list of chores for us to do and be done by the time they got home from work. We had a concrete back porch. When we washed clothes, we would get a whipping if the porch was not dry when they came home. My father's brother lived across the street from us. Daddy would always go over there after work and that's when the beatings would take place.

On Sunday, my sister and I would get up early and walk around the corner to Sunday school. When we got home sometimes, we shared a biscuit and a piece of sausage that was left of breakfast and we had to wash the dishes. Sometimes, our stepmother would not go to the fields with us, and when she found out that we didn't pick over 200 pounds of cotton, she would whip us, saying our daddy let us play and not work.

Our school clothes were made of 25 cent material she had bought and made us dresses (she could not sew at all). We had no choice; it was all we had to wear. We could go nowhere, but sometimes over to our cousin's house on the next street. We had a chinaberry tree in our back yard. That was as far as we could go to play most of the time. We also had an outside toilet.

If wishing something would make it happen, I would have died a long time ago. The outhouse was my wishing place; I wished so many times that I would die, just to get away from all of the abuse and mistreatment. *I know now that God was keeping us, and it was him that didn't let my wish of dying come true. Thank You Lord! I know that God saved me for a reason. I am praying that the Holy Spirit will reveal my work for the Lord to me soon.*

Chapter Two

RUNNING AWAY

My sister Dorothy was much like my aunt, Annie Bell, quite aggressive, mean-spirited, and strong in thought and deed. One day, after a very long day in the field picking cotton with only our father there, we came home. The mean old stepmother didn't go that day. After we had supper, dad took his usual trip over to Uncle Johnny's house across the street. The devil jumped right in the mean-spirited stepmom, and she made us get a rake and rake the yards. Mind you, we had been in the fields all day, picking cotton. The Georgia sun was approximately 96 degrees, so hot you could see heat waves in the air. We were exhausted! And she made us rake the yards, all the while we did it she complained that, "Y'all didn't pick enough cotton today, I am going to whip your asses, your daddy let you play instead of working." We became quite scared; this was to be another of her beatings for no reason. My sister had a light go on in her head and she said, "She ain't gonna beat me today, I am going to get daddy." As I was quite passive and afraid at the time she said, "Are you going with me?" I replied, frightened, "Yes, you ain't gonna leave me here by myself." Quickly we eased around the house and slipped over across the street to Uncle Johnny's house where our father was. My sister being the leader that she was said, "Daddy, daddy. She is making us rake the yard, and she says she is gonna beat us because we didn't pick enough cotton."

That night in the bed we quietly planned our runaway because my sister said she was not gonna take any more beatings. Her next move made me more afraid, she said, "Are you going with me?" Frightened beyond reproach, I replied, "Yes! If you go you are not leaving me here." As we drifted off to sleep, I thought I don't want to leave my daddy as I loved my daddy very much. I had to make a decision if I were to stay there with my father and continue to be treated less than a child or human being or run away with my sister. By morning my decision was made. I knew my sister was firm in her decision, so I had to be as well. We began our plan!

First, we would write our oldest brother in Americus, Pap, as he was affectionately called, and ask him if we could come live with him and his wife, Jessie Bell. We would explain the physical abuse we suffered, and the fact that we wanted to finish high school. At the rate we were going, we would not finish. All our stepmother wanted us to do was pick cotton. As she was illiterate, she didn't want us to be educated. However, our father wanted us to be educated. My dad was good in math; he could say his timetables fast. Education for my sister and I was important to him.

In Cordele, Georgia a small southern town, they would publish the names of children who made the honor roll. When my name would appear in the paper, I felt very proud to show it to my dad. He would be proud, too. At this time, I was in the 7th grade and my sister was in the 9th grade. My sister's name didn't appear; however, she was smart in math, a trait she took from her dad. I guess this was self-learned on his part; as a sharecropper he had to know if the white boss man was paying him correctly for the people he brought to the fields to do the hard labor work, and he would not be cheated.

If you know anything about southern Georgia states, you will know the weather is very hot in June. The cotton was right for picking, and no one had invented the automatic cotton picker yet! Dorothy and I were fighting to plan our end of school escape. We began to pack what clothes we had in a box and shove it to the back of our closet. Our plan was to get daddy to let us go to school the last day of school, and have our brother be at the house about 3:15 to pick us up. Our goal was to leave as fast as possible. The days ahead for me created a series of mixed emotions. My inner thoughts were, first, how much I loved my daddy and I didn't want to leave him. I didn't understand why he allowed this woman to abuse us, or, if he really knew all the times she did it would he have intervened as he did when we didn't pick enough cotton to her taste. Leaving home was another mysterious emotion baffling me. However, one thing was sure: I was not going to let my aggressive sister leave me there to be further victims of an abusive stepmother. While my sister was the oldest, she was also the strongest. Sister Dorothy was mean, strong willed, and could fight.

My sister and I ran away from home at my age of 14, my sister was 16 years of age. We went to live with my oldest brother (Pap) as he was affectionately called, and his wife Jessie Bell (or should I say JEZEBEL, and that she was.) They had no children, but would later adopt one of her sisters' children from Philadelphia. This began a whole new chapter of memorable events in our lives. If the old proverbial saying of "jumping out of the skillet into the fire", was ever truthful, this was it!

This was also a small country southern town, 32 miles from our birthplace of Cordele, Georgia. This was the town of Americus, Georgia, surrounded by red clay. When it rained, you would get red clay all over your shoes that was very difficult to get off. In later years, the demographic structure of this town would change drastically, from a small, beautiful country town surrounded by much greenery and fishponds and the Flint River to a larger urban city. This was largely due to the fact that in an even smaller city named Plains, Georgia, on a peanut farm, a young European male would become President of the United States of America!

Plains is 9 miles from Americus. Who would think that a peanut farmer would become President of the United States? Well, he did, and his term only lasted his four years, of which much comedy from society was verbalized. His wife and his daughter, who was young at the time, grew up in the White House and Oval Office. Her formal education was at the Woodward Academy. Amy was taken from a small country school into the limelight of a very prestigious school. Wow! What an adjustment for her.

Now my sister-in-law had a good-hearted side and a bad-hearted side. I learned much later that she was older and more financially stable than my brother, whom we called "Pap." When she was alright with him, she was alright with my sister and me. When she was mad at him, she was mad at us. There were times when her anger at him, caused her to put us out in the rain, with our clothes in boxes on our heads, heading down the street to our second oldest brother's house, who then lived in the projects with his four children. *Thank God* we could go there and stay until she was no longer angry at Pap. When they were no longer angry, she would call us home.

Jessie was the head chef at a restaurant downtown owned by a Sicilian white man named George Siliba. Mr. George was a big man with a kind heart. Jessie was an excellent cook and *thank God we were never hungry again.* Most of the time, she would bring food home from her workplace, so we always had plenty to eat. We also had a chance to work part time with her and began to make some spending money. In the beginning, we still went to the fields to pick cotton, but after a while we were allowed to work with her instead of going to the field. *Thank God for that.*

After our runaway from home, we didn't go back to Cordele for a long time. Actually, Jessie had to force us to go back. You see, they would go to Cordele every Sunday to see daddy. When it was time for them to go, my sister and I would leave home until after they left. Our first visit back was good in that I missed my daddy and was glad to see him, but I was mostly afraid of his wife. We knew she could no longer abuse us physically and that we were no longer in her control.

High School in Americus

9th grade to 12th High School Graduation:

My formal education was very difficult, with first having interruptions going back and forth to Atlanta for operations and the teasing I experienced from my peers. The poison that I had swallowed had burned my mouth, inside and outside, my throat and down into my right lung. My lips were burned, and black spots were very visible. This gave way to teasing by peers who alleged that I had been smoking cigarettes and burned my lips. My bottom lip remains swollen and puffed out until this day. I also received teasing from peers about me dipping snuff, an old southern cultural thing similar to chewing tobacco or dipping snuff. This was done by older Negroes and whites for comfort. Later it gave way to modern cigarette smoking and ballplayers chewing tobacco.

We were enrolled in school and for the first time ever, got new clothes to wear to school. Jezebel, my sister-in-law, had a charge account at a downtown shop called the Diana Shop. For the first time in our lives, we knew what it was like to have new clothes for school, and we could go and pick out our clothes and charge them to her account. Also, for the first time we were in style with our peers.

My sister and I would be in our high school years of education. In 1962 my sister, Dorothy and I transferred from A.S. Clark High in Cordele, Georgia to Sumter County High in Americus, Georgia. This was the year my sister didn't get promoted. So, instead of being two grades ahead of me, I caught up one grade behind her. Dorothy would repeat the 10th grade and I would get promoted to 9th grade.

In Georgia in the 50's & 60's there was nothing known as "Social promotion." If you didn't pass a grade, you simply repeated it until you did. This process would be beneficial in today's society to better prepare our young people for college.

Sumter County High School located on the colored side of town, on Rucker Street a few blocks from home, which was 1417 North Lee St. In Americus, Georgia the demographic structure of the city was Black people lived north Lee Street, and White people lived South Lee Street. You had to know the boundaries of the city; when you crossed over to South Lee Street, then you knew you were in the white folk's territory.

Adjustment to a new school, new classmates, and new teachers were all difficult. Sumter County High School was all black, located on the black side of the city. Children were bused in from surrounding County Towns, such as Plains, Georgia (The Home of President Jimmy Carter, only 9 miles away), Leesburg, Ellaville, Buena Vista and other county areas around Americus.

Although the integration law, "Brown vs. Board of Education" had passed in 1955, southern schools were not integrated until 10 years later. Approximately 1966, Americus, Georgia experienced its first school integration. Although I graduated and moved off to college in the fall of 1965, I still heard of the integration dynasty of Americus:

"Author Andrew Billingsly wrote a novel entitled "Black family in America." This book would describe my 4 years of high school at Sumter County High. Classes were of small size, no more than 15-20 students per class. At graduation time, the entire graduation class of 1965 was only 200 in numbers.

Teachers in those days were serious about education and parents were not concerned about teachers abusing children, only that they were learning or getting an education.

When school started, we were with a whole new set of peers and teachers.

Our counselor was a nice quiet man who dealt with us mildly. The counselor was instrumental in assisting us with the transfer. One day I was coming down the hallway and to my surprise there he was in Americus at Sumter County High. We talked briefly and then he was gone.

There was our Chemistry and Physics teacher who always drank ice water during class time. Already old at the time I was in school, she was still alive at our 10th year class reunion. We invited her, but she was unable to come, but sent us a nice note. Her husband was an old white man barber downtown; she was a very light complexion black woman.

Then there was our English teacher. English was my best subject. This teacher was a tall thin man who had a very aggressive and strong demeanor. He was a good teacher and he didn't take no mess. I recall one day another student and I were in the back talking and he said "If you all don't be quiet, I will come and throw you out the window." We hushed because we knew he meant it. I would later get an "A" out of a paper I wrote about Walt Disney in his class.

Our history teacher was a big manly looking woman, who was mean on the outside but had a caring heart. I know this because at age 14 I became a woman in her class, and she gave me a Kotex napkin and let me go home to take care of myself. You never came to her class without your homework, she didn't allow that.

Later we would have a big fat man who resembled Santa Clause by the stomach as our teacher. He would sit at his desk, rub his stomach and try to look under the girls' dresses. He was o.k. as a teacher.

Our algebra teacher was soft spoken and mild mannered and was serious about teaching. Most of the teachers back then cared about your learning experience. I know this because algebra was my weakest and most difficult subject. I had to take it twice before I passed it with a grade of "D." As I said, there was no such thing as social promotion at this time. If you didn't pass the course, you had to repeat it. Currently it remains my least liked subject. My sister Dorothy would be good in math, she still is today, after retiring from K-mart as an accountant. Once I moved to Michigan, I used to send her my bank book to balance for me, (my dependence on my big sister, mother).

I tell some of my close acquaintances that my legs are so skinny because back in the day, you went to the blackboard to work the algebra problem and explain it to the class how you got the answer. Every time I didn't get it right; I got a pop on my legs with a small wooden pointer, until I got the answer right.

To this day I don't like anything to do with secretarial work, because of my high school typing teacher. This teacher was funny, and she loved her job. She always called me Sarah Ann, although my name was Sarah Mae. Tall, light skinned with red hair fairly aged, she had a long teaching history. She was tall, thin in stature and well, but dressed comfortably. Our teacher taught typing and shorthand out of the Gregg typing books and the Underwood typewriter with blank alphabet keys. So, you had to learn the alphabets on the blank typing keys. She would walk around the room with her ruler (weapon) in hand, each time you hit the wrong key, she would pop you on the knuckles with the ruler, until you got it right! Shorthand was difficult for me to learn.

One day, I tried to cheat, using Gregg shorthand book, by turning my book upside down to read my sentence in shorthand. Sure enough, she caught me, popped my hand with her wooden pointer and made me write 500 times, "I will not cheat in shorthand class." Today I know how to write my name in shorthand and a few alphabets. "I still dislike secretarial typing stuff."

In the South, teachers (black) were the high-class people, even though they were only allowed to teach in black schools. Teacher's children were also high-class children. Light skin blacks were also high-class. This is the "class within a class" that author Andrew Billingsly speaks of in his famous book mentioned earlier.

Our Physical Ed. Teacher was tall and thought he was cool and handsome. Here is where I learned the game of football. We played a powder-puff game of which I had to sneak and play because Jessie forbade me to play because of my lung and breathing problem. I recall one time during a practice game, I was the center player, and this big girl in class tried to tackle me and pushed me down so hard, we got into an argument that had to be settled by coach. In powder-puff there is no tackling, just touch and she broke the rule.

There was the principal, a little old frail man who smoked cigarettes. He was married, but he was seeing one of the school staff on the side.

The school social worker was a trip. She had her picks and chooses of students she liked and didn't like. She was highfaluting and thought she was high-class. She liked the students whose parents were teachers or principals or in her high-class circle. Of course, I was neither, therefore she didn't particularly care for me. My lifetime friend Johnnie Mae, (Toot as she was called), was very smart, and I wasn't too far behind her, but we were of the poor class of families. This meant that upon graduation the counselor only helped the upper-class students get funding for college, in that their teacher parents or elite blacks could afford some of the money and she helped them get the rest. In my senior year, she helped the so-called elite students with college prep., and told me, "Sarah, you know your father can't afford to send you to college." Although at the time she was right, I pursued it anyway and my daddy did send me to Albany State College for one year and paid cash for it. It is now known as Albany State University, located in Albany, Georgia.

My sister graduated the year president Kennedy was assassinated. When we heard the news, I was on the outside walkway coming from the cafeteria after having lunch. All the students were upset, and my sister had an "I don't care" attitude. Virginia Davis said to me, "Sarah, your sister don't care that the president just got shot?" I said, "So." My sister was only concerned about graduating and getting on with her life and that was o.k. with me.

Willie C. Merritt and her were a couple in high school. In fact, in the yearbook, they were pictured as the most devoted couple. They would go on to be married and he would join the Army and they would move away, leaving me to do my last year in high school alone. I felt very sad about this. They got married at our church on Hampton Street and I was her bride maid. A lot of people didn't want the marriage to happen, but it did. They stayed married 10 years and had a son. Willie C., Bubba as he was called, was a little younger than my sister, but they were in the same grade.

My sister was very bossy and straightforward, I think what went wrong in their marriage was that she didn't allow Bubba to be his own self as a man. Her need to control things led to a very violent divorce. After he was through in the service, they relocated in Atlanta, Georgia with a beautiful home and land large enough to have a horse on grounds. My now adopted sister, Heathie Jenkins-Loveless-Jackson took her first trip to Georgia with me to visit them. My nephew, Spencer Charles Merritt was an infant at the time. My sister would not let us pick him up once she had put him down for the night. We had a wonderful time, back in the day when the "Underground" in Atlanta was really popular.

Chapter Three

SOUTHERN PRE-ADOLESCENCE AND FAMILY

For this chapter you must know something about southern child-rearing to comprehend this. However, there are important lessons to be learned here. My first Childhood crush was with our paper boy, whom I will call Bob. Every day Bob would deliver our paper on his child-built bicycle around the same time in the evening. Most of the time, I would retrieve the paper, with hellos. Bob would respond with words back, smiles and his eyes lighting up. Bob always had extra words to say; however, me being afraid of what my daddy would say if he caught me talking to him, I was always limited with words. As time went on, we had more days of him talking to me and my limited words because of fear from my dad.

As you can gather, I was not good at sneaking talking to boys. Most of the time I spent shooing him away before my dad caught us talking. Bob was persistent in his pursuit of me, and he had no intentions of stopping. My sister (Dorothy) was way more aggressive in her pursuit of romance. Later, I would learn her aggressive behavior was patterned after my dad's oldest sister, as we called her, Aunt Annie Bell, real name, Annie Bell Price.

Aunt Annie Bell was a character that everyone has in their family: she was bossy, aggressive and mean! Aunt Annie Bell bossed everybody, including my daddy. I guess because she was the oldest, she took on the mother role for my dad.

I never knew any of my father's parents; I would later learn their names and some of their behavior patterns. My paternal grandmother's name was Minnie Cobb; my Grandfather's name was Johnny Cobb, a heavyset, angry man. Later I would learn that the Cobb name was our slave given name. In researching the Cobb ancestry, it was revealed to me that the name Cobb is of European decent and Indian heritage. In Cordele Georgia, my birthplace, Caucasians with the name Cobb own a lot of business all over, so I guess they have money. Even as you travel south, you will see a lot of Europeans named Cobb, and it is obvious that they had a lot of inherited wealth. There are all kinds of Cobb insurance agencies, real estate and other businesses throughout Georgia. I am able to say that my heritage had some wealth and that we are descendants of slaves according to my older sibs.

In my mother's birthplace, Americus, Georgia, 32 miles from Cordele, there is a middle school named Sarah Cobb Elementary. My niece's son attended the school and I asked him to inquire about the person the school was named after. All he said was they told him it was named after "some old white lady."

As I am the youngest most of my family history was learned from my older siblings. I learned that Grandma Minnie was quiet and possibly sort of passive in her marriage, as well as a parent. My grandfather Johnny was aggressive and very mean. While my grandmother was dark in complexion, my grandfather was very light in complexion. Out of the twelve children of which ten of us survived, two died very young. Probably because all of us were born at home under the watch of a "MIDWIFE." Blacks were not allowed in hospitals back in the forties. I now know this because I was born at home and my mother got sick after birth and was not taken to the hospital soon enough, so she died after having me.

My favorite uncle, Uncle Bud, as we affectionately called him would later tell me in a drunken stupor that "I killed my mother." I loved him dearly because he could plug in parts of my life that I didn't know about. Prior to his death in the late 1990s I spent a lot of time with him telling me about family history. I miss my uncle very much.

You see, he died hungry. Prior to his death, his stepdaughter, Evelyn, hired her cousin to feed my uncle through a feeding tube. This lady left him with my sister-in-law's (old ma) friend to watch him, but she couldn't feed him because she didn't know how. Upon my arrival my uncle was hungry, and I couldn't feed him either because of the tube inside of him. I rubbed his head, and he threw up his hands for protection. This indicated that someone had been striking him, probably the lady who was supposed to feed him. This person had already been turned away from caring for her own mother, whom she had been paid to take care of. Now if your own mother didn't think you were capable of caring for her, then how can you be hired by the stepdaughter to care for my uncle?

My uncle had a vision of a glass of water and some bread. His words to me were "See? There is a glass of water and some bread, give it to me" and I couldn't because of the feeding tube insert. This was the last time I saw my uncle alive. I left very angry and hurt. The lady sitting with him detected this and contacted my cousin Evelyn. Evelyn called me afterward and we discussed the situation; I suggested she take him back to the hospital. Finally, she did, but too late. My uncle passed away shortly afterward at Riverview Hospital on East Jefferson Avenue in Detroit, Michigan. He went on to be with his wife, who had preceded him in death.

I miss my uncle very much; he was my favorite uncle. As a child in Georgia, I recalled he would always bring my sister and me boxes of clothes when they came to visit us in Georgia. They would always arrive in the early morning hours, and it would be a joyous time for us because we would have a box of new clothes. I later learned that my uncle tried to get my daddy to give him my sister and I after my mother's death.

At first, I didn't understand why he didn't, later I learned that both my uncle and his wife were functional alcoholics, and my cousin, my aunt's daughter was her pride and joy. My daddy probably figured we would be treated like stepchildren over my cousin. Later my cousin would break her mother's heart by going into her bank account and withdrawing all of her life savings and her and her daughter, Cynthia, would spend it for themselves. This of course broke my aunt's heart and I think she lost the will to live. I always remember that when my aunt would introduce my sister and I to her friends she would start by saying, "These are Foster's nieces." Later during her illness, she began calling me on the phone. This was very new to me. I recalled the first call to me from her, I was so surprised and shocked, and I didn't know how to respond, so I did a lot of listening. My aunt went home to be with God, soon after that. My uncle missed her so much; I would visit him often to make sure he was o.k.

Sometimes when I visited, I could tell when he was really missing her as he would have on her house coat. I knew then he was really having a bad day. My uncle's drinking began to escalate. After being married to my aunt for over 45 years I can imagine the loneliness he felt. In the few years that followed, my uncle would request that his female tenant become his legal guardian and put her name on his bank book because he no longer trusted his stepdaughter after what she did to her mother.

I would check on my uncle on my day off (Monday) and Sunday after church. Monday would be for errands and banking. Sunday would be for dinner to make sure he had fixed himself some food. My uncle was southern raised; therefore, he could prepare his own meals, and I had to make sure the grocery was there. He had long stopped driving; I think he was basically illiterate and drove for years without a drivers' license. My uncle could drive really drunk without having an accident.

Somehow when it was time for him to really stop driving, his garage caught fire and burned up with his van in it. Early in his life my uncle drove the car that was every poor black man's dream, a Cadillac.

A Trying Childhood

The long term effects of the poison I swallowed affected my throat, as well as my vocal cords, so since I was an infant, (in crying stage) and was not able to talk for years; my voice stayed at the baby voice I would have had during my development. The Lye (poison) I swallowed had traveled down my throat into my lower right lung. In order for me to recover, they had to remove part of my lung.

If race or prejudice existed within Grady's Memorial Hospital in 1960, I couldn't tell. The nurses were Caucasians, as were the doctors, and I was very well cared for during this final operation at age 14. Mind you, I had numerous surgeries at this same hospital from crawling stage development until age 14.

Later one of my stepsister's would be a nurse at Grady's, and I would try to get records of my stay there. I would be told; after so many years a lot of records were destroyed once they changed how they kept records. Maybe it was best I didn't get records. I don't know how long my recovery was, I do know I was there until I got well. Once I was able to get up and walk around, I visited other children on the ward.

On visiting day, I would sit in a chair by the elevator and watch other family members come for visiting day. Needless to say, each time the elevator opened I was looking for my family. I was the only child who got no family visits, but I did get coloring books, crayons and other small toys or books from hospital staff and visiting family members. I was very thankful to staff and other family members, but I was lonely for my family. Later, I would know that because my dad was poor and his only income was to be the field supervisor, he had to work to make money. The trip was approximately 150 miles from Cordele, Georgia to Atlanta, Georgia so I am sure now time and money played a vital part in my family not coming to visit me.

Time passed and my recovery continued to improve. Bandages were removed and the healing was progressing. One day Dr. Davis came to visit to explain I would be going home soon. Good news! I've already shared how that good news turned into sorrowful news as my mother departed my life.

Having my voice impacted in such a manner gave way also to a lot of mimicking from my baby voice in an adult body. This voice remains with me today; because I am almost seventy-four years of age now, it has matured somewhat. You wouldn't believe some of the comments I still get about my voice.

I have again learned to ignore them or simply not respond to the comments, positive or negative. I do remember 3 (three) comments that people stated, and I will share them with you at this time:

(1) One day in Detroit, Michigan in a grocery store a man behind me heard me talk; his response to me was; "All you would have to do is talk to me in that voice and I would give you anything you wanted." I simply smiled and made no comment.

(2) A Caucasian lady at the Eastern Market in Detroit spice shop heard me talk; her response was, "I have a cousin in Hollywood. If you could record your voice, I would send it to him, and maybe you could make a deal with him." Needless to say this was just talk. I found out because I went back to her the following Saturday for the address of her cousin in Hollywood. I got an address and name. I purchased a recorder and tape, taped a message and sent it off to Hollywood. My message was such that

"Don't try to use my voice without my consent or you'll be in trouble." I never heard from Hollywood;

(3) This one is the most amusing to me. In transacting business over the phone to creditors, etc. once they hear my voice, they begin reciting the "you must be 18 or older" line to me. Second, they ask me my birth date. I give it to them with pride! Even today *I am not reluctant to say how old I am because I am so very thankful to God that I have been kept by his love for me all these years.*

My mother's name is: Etha Mae Coleman-Cobb, at her death and my birth, she was 38 years old. I was told by my oldest brother (Pap) that I looked just like her. The only picture I have of my mother; she is in her casket and I can barely see her face. My father and several people are standing in a half circle around the casket.

All of what I know about my biological mother; I learned from older siblings and my favorite uncle; (Uncle Bud) Foster Ingram was his birth name. In his last year, I spent a lot of time with him, asking questions about my mother, I know for sure that; at age 38 my mother had given birth to 10 children at a time when black babies were delivered at home by midwives. I discovered this by visiting her gravesite in a cemetery outside of Cordele, Georgia; at Gum Creek Baptist Church, noticing on her grave head stone, she was 38 years of age at the time of her death, and my birth.

I further remembered while being with my oldest brother, I was standing at the stove one day as he was telling me something I didn't want to hear, although it was right at age 21 or 22; I didn't want to hear it. Pap stated to me; "You hear what I am saying to you? Standing there looking just like Etha Mae Coleman." By this I felt good that at least, I now knew what my birth mother looked like!

Pap also told me my father beat my mother with a belt. His words were, "As I watched him beat my mother with a belt, I wanted to jump on him and choke the life out of him!! This probably explained my Uncle Wiggins dislike for my father, as does my younger brother's (Arthur L. Cobb, Jr.) mistreatment of his wife who is older than him.

As my favorite uncle (Uncle Bud) was a functional alcoholic, his drunken declarations of "You killed my sister" didn't bother me because; I loved him and knew he didn't understand how serious the birth of a child is. I also was told my mother was not taken to the hospital soon enough after my birth at home.

The last point I recall about my mother was that my father's brother, Uncle Johnny's wife, Aunt Queen used to tell my sister and I to "Keep your panties pulled up, because had your mother listen to me, she wouldn't be in the shape she was in" (Dead). Aunt Queen was blind, so we did a lot of things for her (including writing those letters so we could see the letters from our Mama Lessie) as we lived directly across the street from her.

Lessie Mae Sherman-Cobb was the only mother I knew. Although I never felt anything but love for her, my older sibs talked of her being mean. Momma was very dark in complexion and had a gold tooth. Momma Lessie smoked cigarettes a lot. In 1982 in Titusville, Florida Momma Lessie died of lung cancer. I was completing my bachelor's degree in social work at Wayne State University at the time of her death. When she knew she was dying she called me to come to Titusville, Florida where she lived with a man named Mr. James. My daughter, Heather was 2 years old at the time, and in the middle of being potty trained. I remember catching a bus to Florida with a potty seat top in hand, because I couldn't break the training.

We spent time together at night, where my mom told me things she thought I needed to know. After that we went to the bank, she left me some money, of which she gave me cash, a large amount. Some she gave to me, the other she gave to my brother Silas Cobb, Sr. Mom told me not to buy a car with it, but a car was what I needed most to get back and forth to W.S.U. at the time.

My mother had done domestic work for a rich Caucasian family for a long time. In a hope chest she had a lot of new and expensive things they had given her. Mom said to me, "When I pass, you hurry down here and get this stuff." I didn't get that point because I felt if she truly wanted me to have it, she could have given it to me then. Needless to say, I didn't get it. My mother had a cousin there in Titusville and we would later learn that my mom had made two (2) wills, one which she left her house and other items to me and Silas, and one she left everything to her male cousin. Both wills were made by the same attorney, but years apart and it was unclear as to which one took priority over the other one. The cousin ended up getting everything, which was o.k. with my brother Silas and me.

My father Arthur Lee Cobb, Sr. at the time of my birth, was 38 years of age at least. That was what is on my birth certificate. My father is medium light, with original brown skin, due to his time in the sunlight, as the years rolled on his complexion became darker due to exposure to the hot southern sun. My father was a small frame man with small feet, a deacon in his church and wore Stacy Adam shoes to church. My dad had a handicap left arm, however he could use this arm in relation to helping the right hand do what he needed to do.

This I know well, because he gave me one whipping with his leather belt he wore on his work pants. My stepsister and I found a cigarette butt and tried to smoke it. Our brothers told on us and when my father and his third (3rd) wife returned from the grocery store my father took me in one room, my stepmother took her daughter in another room. My father gave me a really intense whipping with his good hand. I feel that's the reason, I never smoked cigarettes during my adult life.

I was my father's baby girl, I loved him, and I believed he loved me. Although he never said, "I love you", he eventually displayed it in a nonverbal way. I later learned that his father was a very mean, angry, red-skinned man, who probably never said the "I love you" words to him.

My father was a firm disciplinarian; he ruled his household with strength. My older brother's (males) were taught work ethics by him and the (2) two girls, my sister and I, were taught education. My father was a sharecropper, who worked for his Caucasian employees, where he took field hands to the field daily, was paid per head, (.50 per head), and whatever else was worked out between him and his then "Boss" because this was in a slavery mode. My father was also responsible for making sure that whatever work was to be done, the field hands were to do it, under my father's supervision. My father had (2) two trucks which he used to transport his field hands.

Cotton was the first crop we were involved in. The time was 6:00 am-6:00 pm/6 days a week. Chopping cotton was first, then picking it at $3.00/lb. once cotton season was over. We were loaded on my father's truck with the back part covered. I will never forget the plantation we lived on in Belle Glade Florida. The four children and the wife of the day went to a place called Belle Glade. In Belle Glade, the dirt is black and called "muck." We actually lived on a "plantation." This was in the 60's in the south.

My father must have had a contract of some kind with the Caucasian man, who owned the plantation. The buildings were set up all alike. They were grey in color and all the families stayed in one cabin. We were six in number, one bed for the children, one for the adults. I remember my sister and I slept at one end of the bed and my (2) two brothers slept at the other end. These cabins were set back off of a main highway with a store up front and it was a bus stop for school children to catch the bus to school.

This crop was string beans; the time of year was fall. There was a truant officer assigned to this plantation to visit the bean fields to see if any children were there instead of going to school. Our father hid us from the truant officers so that we could work. I will never forget us being hid from the truant officer when he came to the field to look for children who were supposed to be in school.

Our meals consisted of beans from the field and cornbread. I remember one day a lady that worked at the school brought us some food she had left over. This was the only real meal I recall us having. Back in Georgia there were pecans to be picked up in the wintertime. We had to crawl on our knees to pick up the pecans and it was very cold. At times we were allowed to build a small fire to warm our hands and body. This was our way of surviving.

The morning dew caused the string beans to be wet, early in the morning. Therefore, we had to wait awhile for the beans to dry before we could pick them.

If you've ever been to Belle Glade Florida or Delray Beach, you will know about the small streams of water called "Canals." Canals lead to the big river and often had alligators, snakes and other water animals in them. When we weren't hiding from the truant officer, a group of us would play jumping over the Canals. They were small enough for you to jump over.

This is where I learned a valuable lesson about listening to my elders and being obedient. As we played, an elderly lady said to us, "You kids better stop jumping over those Canals, there are alligators in there." My not listening, nor being obedient, I had to do it one more time. I knew in my mind (or I thought) I could make the jump across. The process was to back up first, then run and stretch your legs to be able to jump across to the other side! Again, I knew I had it made.

Little did I know then, my disobedient behavior would almost cost me my life. This section of Florida is called wetlands. I backed up to a few steps and jumped, my foot landed over the Canal but in the soft edge and before I knew what happen, I was in the Canal yelling, "Help Dorothy (my sister)." *By the grace of God she was able to grab me by the hand and pull me out of the Canal.* As you know once you hit the water alligators smell human flesh, so they come to eat what they smell.

My father didn't discipline me about this, I guess he figured how scared I was, was discipline enough. I had to wear my wet clothes until they dried. Lesson learned about obeying the elderly. And I never learned to swim due to my fear of drowning. I would later take a beginners swimming class at Wayne State University as I was obtaining my Bachelor of Social Work Degree. I had an instructor who knew my fear of drowning and was patient with me. Once I finished the course, which was an elective, I never went back to swimming class.

Today, I don't care for string beans, because on the plantation that's all we had for dinner - string beans and "hot water cornbread." "Hot water cornbread is a southern delicacy." When I say we were poor as we grew up, I mean it. However, my father being the strong individual he was, we were never without what we "needed." How much of what we needed is another question? There was a lady on the plantation that worked as a cook in a school. Once she was able to bring leftover food from the kitchen to share with us. Mac & cheese and some kind of meat. I don't remember what, but this was a feast compared to string beans and hot water cornbread. This lady could have been one of my father's concubines of which he had many! At the time, my mother (thinking she was my real one) Lessie Mae Sherman was the 2nd wife.

It later became clear to me why my daddy had four (4) wives. Arthur Lee Cobb Sr. loved women and sex. I suppose he used his manhood desires to relieve his stress related to survival both economically and the fact that he had a limited amount of education. This gave way to his child rearing rules of wanting his 2 girls to be educated, and his 8 boys to work and take care of their families, as he did the best he could. My daddy ruled his household in a firm, mild-mannered quiet way. I remember a lot of quiet time we spent sitting on the front porch, with us on the steps and daddy in his easy chair.

As my sister and I were teenagers and begin to get interested in the opposite sex, my sister, the brave one between us, decided one day to ask daddy when she could have Boy Company. My daddy didn't hesitate to answer her; he said simply, "When you get 18." That was the end of the boy subject. I, of course, dare not ask with me being two years younger, and the baby girl. I had no chance of getting even that kind of answer. So, I didn't ask. Instead, we both began to "sneak" and talk to boys without our father's knowledge. In the south around the late fifties, it was a custom in school for the sexes to write letters to each other if they "liked" someone.

Chapter Four

YOUNG RELATIONSHIPS VS ADULT RELATIONSHIPS

Once we ran away to Americus to live with my brother (Pap) and his wife (Jessie). We were in high school and our female hormones had heightened to spark an interest in the males we were associated with.

My first interest was with a boy named Curtis Simpson! Curtis was short like myself, brown complexion, a little heavy but to me was handsome! Most of all, he was interested in me, and worked with my brother Pap at Barnum Funeral Home in Americus, Georgia. Curtis had a black and white old model car; I think I liked to ride in the car better than keeping company with him. Our relationship went on at least a year because at Christmas time he bought me a fake diamond ring and I bought him a brown V-neck pullover sweater.

Shortly after that he found a girl that would be sexually active with him and I wasn't about to be. First, because I didn't know how and second, I wasn't interested in having sex. Our relationship ended, however we still spoke to each other when we crossed paths, often as he was still working with my brother at the local funeral home.

My brother Pap worked for Grandma, who at the time owned and operated the funeral home with helpers such as my brother. My brother's formal education was minimal; however, he was a favorite of Grandma. His main job was to go wherever within the surrounding cities that needed funeral service to pick up the deceased person and bring them back to the funeral home. Curtis and one other young man were his helpers.

Pap's second job was to collect the rent of houses in and around Americus that was owned by Grandma's son. He was a functional sometime alcoholic. Married with two boys and one girl, his wife taught biology at the local black high school. Grandma has one daughter who helped with the business.

My second relationship in Georgia was with a much younger man Leroy (Lee). Lee was the younger brother of a then friend of mine (Mae Mae) who was a police officer in Americus, Georgia. At the time, she was one of the first black police officers in this small southern town. Jimmy Carter was the president at this time. Officer Mae Mae gave the then President's brother a ticket for DUI. This made the Americus Time Recorder. Officer Mae Mae left Americus, moved to Atlanta and became a GBI, where she worked until years later; she was terminated for not saying she had a substance abuse problem and didn't ask for help.

Lee and I worked for Fred V. Gentch Corp. He was attached to his mother's umbilical cord and we wanted him to be released from his mother's cord and be a man. Our relationship grew until we both were a couple and very much in love. The Vietnam Conflict was active. We talked Lee into joining the Army; we thought it would make a man out of him, so he went in.

My home life was in disarray, so I left Georgia, and asked his sister to explain to him why I wouldn't be in Georgia when he got out. Well, he came home and was suffering from PTSD. He got involved with my niece. Her mother tried to let her know Lee was my mate. My niece didn't care, she continued the relationship. Lee was tall, dark and handsome. He played basketball in high school and he was good at the sport and popular.

I found out he and my niece were involved as I returned to Georgia in the future. I brought them both together. My niece said nothing. When I asked Lee, "Why?" he simply said, "Well, I had to have someone." He later married someone else and stayed with her until her death. I went to church with my sister Dorothy. She and Lee belonged to the same church. At this time, he had become a deacon in his church. As he passed out the song books, he saw me. I went to the bathroom. As I came out, he was standing there waiting for me. He opened his arms, and I went to him, he said, "My baby." We did nothing else as his wife was in the sanctuary in the minister's area.

My final relationship in Georgia began when I was a senior in High School and age 17. Eddie Leon Bryant, Jr. was the adopted son of Eddie Senior and Vivian Bryant. The Bryants were what you would call the "High Class" Black Family. The Bryants owned a business downtown and was quite successful. It included a pool hall, restaurant and later a flour shop. Eddie Sr. was known as a "womanizer" and so was Eddie Jr. I was age 17 and Eddie Jr. had completed college at Mississippi State and had returned home to help with the family business.

The relationship culture in this small southern town and in the black community consisted of the males did the chasing until they caught the girl they wanted. Well, Eddie started chasing me and I started to run away because he had a reputation with other women, and it was said around town he had fathered some children. We had a sundae shop where the high school kids like to hang out after school and on the weekend. Eddie would show up there and chase me around until I would leave the shop. I eventually gave in and he and I had a long relationship.

This continued until after I graduated high school and went off to college. Prior to my going off to college, the summer of 1965-66. I got involved with SNCC (Student non-violent Coordinating Committee). This was my first experience with demonstrating and ending up in city jail for nine days trying to integrate the Then; the Martin Theaters. My family was upset because my plans were to go off to college.

It was a long hot summer and when SNCC came to Americus I was first; Tired of going in the back door of the theater, I wanted to enter the front like the Caucasians did. This was nine (9) days of my life I won't forget. I vowed to myself once I was released I would continue to fight for freedom, but I would do something else other than go to jail.

The feeling of being locked up and not being able to go sit on the porch is quite stressful to the mind. When we were released, I walked from the jail which was downtown past the black and white line of Americus to my house. I didn't want a ride. I wanted to feel what it was like not to be locked up. Later in life I would experience locked up in a totally different way when I started working in a large prison in Detroit, Michigan. I'll share that later ...

Eddie knew about Lee and me, and he liked to refer to Lee that "Our woman is home." I loved both of them and they loved me. Eddie wasn't married, but he was a womanizer. I didn't care about that because I knew where I stood in his life.

I will never forget either of my Georgia relationships and the love we shared with each other. I learned that we could never go back, because of how our lives had been separated, they both will always have a space in my heart!

Lee's wife became ill and stayed ill a long time before her death. Lee was on psychotropic meds for his PTSD. While his wife was alive she could make sure he took them and he would be stable with visits to the VA. After her death, of course he stopped taking what he called "the blue pill" and he would go backward.

We would talk on the phone, I could tell by our conversation he was not taking his meds. By me being a mental health clinician, I could tell he was going backward. So, I stopped trying to talk to him. We sent pictures to each other and that was the extent of our relationship. *Lee had a daughter and sisters who I prayed would help take care of him and not just get his money.* Finally, our relationship ended because I was in the north and he was still in the south.

Shortly after that, Eddie's father passed away. He and his Dad was very close. They had a wake at their home. I didn't go because I couldn't stand to see the hurt on his face. I told my friend to tell him why I didn't come. Later he would come to me, pick me up in his '65 Mustang of which he tried to learn me to drive with the stick shift (it didn't work). He took me to the cemetery to show me where they had buried his father. *I prayed for his loss and we both became emotional.*

Shortly after this, he was called to Mississippi State to teach. He came by to tell me goodbye. I will never forget our time together for this moment. His stay was short at the college because he had to come home and help his mother run the business. I was still up North and would come home periodically. He belonged to another church (Campbell Chapel). One day as I was with my sister at her and Lee's church, he showed up. After service, he came to me, gave me a big hug and said, "My baby." My sister, Dorothy, said to him, "You never hugged me." He said, "You are not my baby." Eddie liked to make Lee jealous by being there with me.

This would be the last time I saw him alive. He and one of the funeral home grandsons got in trouble with the law. The grandson went to prison, but Eddie did not go. His mother was a very sophisticated and rich woman. This probably kept him out of prison. After this we would just talk. His mom became sick and passed away. This hurt him, as he was adopted from New York and he was her baby.

Eddie was much older than me, I guess that's why he tried so much to have me. They had a male group called "The Royal Magnets." Once I came home, he simply came over and said, "Get ready. I'll be back to get you." Of all of his women, to my surprise he was taking me to their annual party. So I dressed up in my up north best dress and waited to be picked up. To everyone's surprise when we walked into the party together. We sat at our reserved table and began our night together. I didn't know that Eddie drank so much. When time came to take me home he had one of his brothers in the club to take me home, given me the keys to his car, and he would walk to my house to get them.

The car was parked in our driveway. Everybody thought he spent the night with me. However, that would not happen at my oldest brother's house where I was staying. My brother had to have his car moved from the driveway so he could get out and go to work.

I had a hard time operating the standard shift gear car, but I finally remembered what he had tried to teach me about driving it (no automatic). I got it pulled to the street in front of the house. The next day, he came to get it, we talked and he went to work at his mother's business.

Later, he married the young girl, who had taken care of his mother. I learned later from him that his mother had told him to marry her, because she was young and she would take care of him. They began to run the business together. Later, I would return to Americus again. This time my daughter would be a teenager. I introduced her to him and he sent us (my niece and I) a bottle of wine to our table. We talked and our love for each other was still there! Little did I know this would be the last time I would see him alive. Eddie Jr. passed away. Now, when I go home it doesn't seem right that he is not there anymore.

Chapter Five

ADULT RELATIONSHIPS IN MICHIGAN

I chose this one, wrong one! I chose him after the long car ride with him from Georgia to Michigan with all my belongings in the car and my brother (Arthur Jr.) following us with a hitch carrying both of their motorcycles attached to his big Oldsmobile car.

We talked all the way here and by the time we got here I had decided I wanted to be his girl. "Wrong thing to do." Reason being, he was married with children. He was separated, but not divorced. He also had a lot of other women. He and my brother were motorcycle brothers. I didn't care at the time, I wanted to be with him, and for eight (8) years we were together. My brother objected. However, it didn't matter to me at the time. *I was operating in my worldly sense, not in my spiritual sense.*

He helped me learn how to drive on freeways and taught me a lot of northern habits. Little did I know I should have left him alone as my brother wanted. So, my brother threatened him to stop seeing me. So, I told him, "You be afraid of my brother." "I am not!" So, I kept seeing him every chance I got. He took me to Belle Isle to show me the deer, of which I had never seen. Sometimes he acted more like a brother to me than a lover. So, we continued on in the relationship until in 1973 I became pregnant. We had an awesome time during my pregnancy. My hormones would act up and I would demand him to get me things, which he did. Once I threw a glass of water at him and he threw one back at me.

By now, he took me to my sister-in-law's house and told them to keep me. Just call him when the baby was born. Nevertheless, in my sixth month of pregnancy, I fell down some stairs in my apartment building. My girlfriend and I laughed because I bounced down the flight of stairs. By midnight I began to have a terrible pain. My friend (Heathie) and I called my gyn who told us to meet him at the hospital (Hutzel Hospital). My doctor examined me and said, "It's much too soon for you to have this baby." He gave me a shot to stop the labor pains. However, the baby came anyway. It was a boy, who died shortly afterward.

This was the first and only time I questioned my heavenly father, "Why, God, did my baby die?" Little did I know then that I should never question God. I cried so hard. When I came home from the hospital my friend Heathie had a gift for me. We were all sad that I had lost the baby. I donated his body to Wayne State University (WSU) to do research about miscarriages in birth. I was working for DPS at the time. All my colleagues were sad for me because they knew how much I wanted the baby.

I almost lost my mind after that. His father was sad, too. He said, "Don't worry, we will get another baby." *I turned to God and asked for His help. I told God if He gave me another child that I wouldn't love it so much; that if it didn't live, I would be alright with it.*

Three years later, I was pregnant again. With this child I was sick almost every day. I had heartburn so bad. I even threw up when I drank water! Old people said it was a girl and that it had a lot of hair and they were right. I didn't speak to my brother (Arthur) the whole time I was pregnant. In 1977, my daughter kept me in labor for 24 hours. My gyn had to give me a shot to help me deliver her. Well, she came, but they had to pull her out of me because her head was so big, she had trouble coming out. They doused my middle section with something very cold.

She finally came out at 1:55 pm on Tuesday, March 1ˢᵗ, 1977. Once they brought her to me to feed her, the nurse came in, took one look at her and took her to ICU. I had no idea what was going on. Later, I would learn that she had jaundice. My gyn came to me to explain what they had to do. She had her father's blood type, not mine, and her body couldn't hold heat. So, they had put her in an incubator, covered up her eyes, so that the light in her incubator would not affect her sight.

The doctor explained that this should correct the problem. If it didn't, they would have to drain her blood and refill her with my blood type. Her hemoglobin needed to be 13. So, I didn't get any sleep that night. I walked back and forth to the nursery all night until the doctor said, "Ms. Cobb, you need to get some sleep. She will be alright." *At this time, I began to pray to God for her health.*

After three days I was discharged home. My baby had to stay to finish her treatment. I felt so sad. *I went home and began to pray and prepare for her to come home.* One week later I was on the phone talking to my friend (Muriel) when the doctor buzzed in and said, "Ms. Cobb, are you ready to come get your baby?" I hung up quickly and called my friend (Olivia) to come take me to get my baby. This day I will never forget. The teacher I worked with at DPS had bought her a pretty go home outfit from Jacobson's Department Store. 1977 was a very cold year. Olivia came to get me to take me to the hospital to bring my baby home. This was one of the happiest days of my life. *(I began to thank God then and haven't stopped yet.)*

In the hospital, they showed me videos about taking care of her. This was my first and last baby and I knew nothing about taking care of a baby. I had borrowed a basinet from my friend (Maxine) to care for her. Her dad had called me from work every night before she was born. He was working at Ford Motor Company at the time, and he would call me on his lunch hour to see how I was doing. The exact night I went to the hospital to have her, he didn't call me. My brother (Silas) was with me for the birth. He was Mr. Cobb, and I was Ms. Cobb. The staff assumed he was the father. He walked with us as they rolled me and the baby to the door to go home. My brother said, "Look at the big head on her, full of hair." Silas Sr., my brother, had brought me a pretty pink and white shoe filled with pink roses. I think he was as happy as I was that she was alright and going home.

Well, after I got home, all my DPS staff was glad to stop by and see her. She weighed only four (4) pounds and some ounces but was very pretty with a big head of curly hair. I was glad to show her, but I could hardly walk to the door to let them in. The hospital had given me a lot of books telling me how to take care of her. One of my friends (Ella) came over and told me to throw those books away. I will show you how to bathe and take care of your baby. Ella had raised two boys. Ella, deceased now, was from Alabama and had raised her two boys by herself. We laughed and she helped me give Heather her first bath. My baby was named after my friend and spiritual sister whose name was Heathie. Heather is a pretty, purple flower. I gave her her middle name, Shantelle.

When the principal of the school where I worked held her she was then five pounds and some. As she held her she said, "Ms. Cobb, she is like a five-pound bag of sugar." We laughed. The principal didn't have any children. Later, I would assist the principal and her husband in adopting a son as I worked at an agency that did adoptions. I was then a Bachelor of Social Work from Wayne State University in Detroit, Michigan.

Somehow her father found out we were home. When I opened the door for him he said, "I ought to whip your ass." "Why didn't you tell me the baby was home?" I told him, "You didn't call me the night she was born so I decided you didn't need to know. If you touch me I'll tell my brothers and they will whip your ass." That ended that. He was very supportive after that. He had a Sicilian godfather who owned a store on Mack Ave. He told him anything I needed for the baby to let me have it. Frank was a very nice man and cared for Curtis a lot as a son.

Well, after I got my master's degree, Curtis wanted me to continue to get my Ph.D. When I said, "I will if you pay for it" that ended that. I had paid Sallie Mae for my masters and it took me seven (7) years, paying $50.00 a month, to complete that.

When Heather was two (2) years old, Curtis came to me and said, "You don't care for me, you only wanted a baby." Well, he was wrong, by this time I was deeply in love with him. However, he had other plans. So, he used the excuse that, "If I don't get out of your life you can't do what you need to do." He left Heather and me when she was two years old although he reminded me that I could get whatever Heather needed from Frank.

My heart was utterly broken, but there was nothing I could do. I grieved for a long time because the man I loved had just walked out of my life and his two-year-old daughter, not realizing he was never mine but was still married and separated from his wife. I also didn't think he was actually leaving me to be with one of his other women.

Life went on for myself and the baby and my professional life continued to take dramatic turns. Years after vowing not to get put in jail I began working in a large prison in Detroit, Michigan for nine years until I retired. (That full experience is another book!) No, I was not an officer. My title was SAD (Special Activity Director). Wow!! My job was to solicit volunteers from the community to come in and provide programs for the inmates. Also, to be a liaison between the community and the prison. I also had to orientate the volunteers to the policy about coming in the facility, have their ID taken, and do background checks on the volunteers.

This called for the need of an outside line in my office so I could schedule the volunteers to come into the facility. I also had to attend several meetings in Lansing, Michigan concerning the service the volunteers would provide; such as, N.A. and A.A. meetings, CSC and Educational services all in connection with the inmates making a successful transition into the community once they were released. I had problems getting a line in my office until the warden stepped in and gave me an outside line. No one was supposed to know this, however, the Deputy of Programs' secretary let the staff know that I had an outside line. This created another problem. Every staff had a key to my office. One day I came into my office and found a furniture bill on my desk. It was from the school's secretary; She had used my phone to call and check on her furniture and to call her son at home to wake him up to go to his job.

After this the phone was cut off and I was told that I could use the Deputy of Programs' phone. This was a problem. I also had problems with giving orders to the officers who were to take the volunteer's pictures. I wrote memos, made phone calls to the sergeant and the captains and the volunteers often had to come in on a schedule because they had to be back at work.

The officers had problems taking orders from me because they only took orders from their commanders such as sergeants and captains, none of which responded to my memos or phone calls because I was not a born in corrections person. In order to get my job done I had to become aggressive with the sergeants and captains. Eventually I would get it done. "Lord, have mercy on me." In order to complete my tasks, I needed the support of the officers.

I went through this time after time, finally I would reach one captain that would assist me. He was the afternoon captain and the officers were obedient to him, so that solved that problem.

Every year the facility was judged for programs by five (5) persons from other states, who came in to view the programs and give the facility an OK. I was able to provide so many positive volunteers that the team wanted to talk to me about how I did it. Of course, the facility took the credit, not me. The team wanted to go back to their state and implement the same program. During my tenure, this facility got its first O.K. from the licensing team!

Leaving a professional agency (Dept. of Mental Health) and coming to a Department of Security, where no professionals were, was very stressful. However, *I prayed to stay there because I was entering my years of retirement and I didn't want any interruptions in my state time. With prayer and supplication, I was able to stay there until I retired at the age of 62.* Other things that went on between me and staff is another book. My *heavenly Father kept me there until retirement. "Thank you, God."*

Upon retiring I stated, I don't want no go away or sendoff. I just wanted to GO! My then warden came to my office one day and said, "Ms. Cobb, we don't want you to go." I said, "But warden, it's time and I have to go." Reluctantly, he said, "Well, if you have to go, then go." I would learn later from my supervisor that because I didn't want a sendoff, I was getting him in trouble. I didn't care because he and his supervisory skills were a great part of why I wanted to go!!

I ate my lunch about 4 pm in the front breakroom with some of the good officers. Little did I know, they had planned a sendoff for me! My daughter, spiritual sister and my newborn grandson showed up to my happy surprise. The good officers had a cake and food from the inmate kitchen. To my surprise, my supervisor showed up, all smiles. I think my facial expression showed him that I didn't want him there. Pictures were taken and I have a video tape done by one of the "good" officers.

Part of my job was also to supervise the "contractors" who came in to give substance abuse training to the inmates. "That's another book." So, I left. *At age 62 I retired, Thank God.*

The second relationship in Michigan was my longest (28 years) and more than I care to go into at this time. Maybe in the next book I will share the blessings that entails. Before I leave the relationships part of this story though I must say this: Curtis James Stringer, Jr., now deceased, came back when Heather was in 12th grade and attending Cass Technical High School. After being gone approximately sixteen (16) years, my knowledge of his return happened downtown at Murphy Hall Court. I had been called to jury duty this summer day. As we waited to get started with the process, the intercom announced if anybody had parked on the street, they needed to move their cars onto the paying lot or they would get a ticket or be towed.

So, a bunch of us headed downstairs to move our cars. As I walked to the elevator, push the down button. I was forever surprised. Who was the first person I saw? Curtis, after sixteen years, my heart flipped. We both were surprised. We talked briefly and agreed to meet outside once I was through with the selection process. Wow! Did I pray I would not be picked for jury duty and I could go meet Curtis. I was working at the prison at the time and I convinced the defendant's attorney that I could not be unbiased because I worked with inmates. Well, my prayer was granted, I was dismissed. I hurried outside where Curtis was waiting on me sitting on the steps.

My emotions were operating in several different stages. Ex. Anger, happiness, surprise and lastly, "What are you doing here?" Well, one of his sons was killed and the suspect was in court for his hearing. He was disgusted about the outcome. I think the suspect didn't get the charge that Curtis wanted.

We talked and we would eventually meet again. He did ask about his daughter. I said we would talk later, however, she is graduating from high school soon and I need a lot of finances. Of course, his conscience thought he could buy her love back with money and material things, such as a car in high school.

Well, he did begin to buy back his lost years of fatherly love. I was focused on class ring, trip, cap and gown, yearbook, etc. His focus was a car. At this time, he had a lawn car service and was very progressive with it. He had city contracts, Chrysler contract, etc. Business was good for him at the time. Curtis bought Heather an old 1988 Oldsmobile, blue and white, of which we named "Big Buford." Heather was not ready to be responsible for a car and she didn't care for Big Buford. The only joy it brought her was about eight of her classmates at Cass Tech could ride in Big Buford at the same time.

Nevertheless, all of them being teenagers cared nothing about checking oil, gas, etc. All they did was ride! One day, "Big Buford" stopped on the freeway. She called me at work, 30 miles from home at Northville Psychiatric Hospital where I was working. I told her to call her father because he was out doing contracts and he was closer to her than I was.

Well, she called him, and of course he rescued her!! Later he called me to tell me that "Big Buford" had no oil and no gas in her. After that she didn't want the car anymore, so her father took it and gave it to one of her brothers (his sons).

Upon graduation, Heather and her dad teamed up against me for her to attend Eastern Michigan University. Her father's reason was, "If she needed something, she was close so we could get it to her." My choice was Michigan State. Heather's actual choice was an HBCU college in the south. I wasn't paying out of state fees when there were good colleges here.

When the time came for her to go to college, her auntie Ella Jean (now deceased), her Aunt (Heathie) and I loaded our three cars up with supplies and we were off to Eastern. I was working at Northville Psychiatric Hospital in Northville, Michigan at the time. As this was her first time away from home, she wanted to be picked up on Friday and taken back on Sunday. That meant I didn't get much rest. I would leave Northville on Friday, go to Ypsilanti, pick her up, and on Sunday after church I would take her back.

I had what I thought was a bright idea that would save me some time and possibly get some much-needed rest. Wow!! Was I mistaken. I bought her a nice used car so she could come home and go back without me. "Big, Big Mistake." Once she got the car, little did I know until much later, that that was the end of school. "That's another book." Maybe I will include it in her legacy.

EPILOGUE

My daughter Heather is now forty-four years old, with a thirteen-year-old male child. Jordon is very technologically oriented, and one day will probably be an IT Technician or own a company where he will teach technology. Now, with being age thirteen (13) and many behavioral issues, he is having problems relating to growing up with the absence of a positive father figure. Jordon was brought up knowing who God is. However, at this stage in his life, he has problems with negative attitudes which equal negative disciplinary actions. He and his mother have to work this out. He is currently in therapy and his church mentoring program. *He knows Ephesians, Chapter Six, Verse 1, which says: "Children obey your parents, for it is right said the Lord."* Only his mother, even at age 44, also has to learn the meaning of this verse as well. *I pray that God will assist both of them in understanding what this verse means.* Jordon asked to be and was baptized in his mother's church. He (Jordon) was in my small church since he was two (2) years old. *So I pray that one day he will realize who God is and that he should look to Him for the help that he needs to control his aggressive behavior. I continue to pray for the both of them: A mother (Heather) raising a child alone and a son (Jordon) learning to be obedient to his mom and all other adults.*

Blessings, Blessings and More Blessings

There are many blessings throughout this book that I pray you have taken notice of.

1. Working for the Board of Education and having them pay for my continued education;
2. Being admitted into the Wayne State University School of Social Work and earning my bachelor's and masters degrees;
3. Working in private agencies as a line staff and supervisor;
4. Being hired by the State of Michigan;
5. And finally, my retirement after such an incredible beginning to life's journey.

Throughout all of life's journey I know that God has been with me and has kept His hand upon me in every situation and turn. There are so many blessings beyond the accomplishments above:

6. Healed from the poison that I swallowed;
7. In the racist South I experienced genuine care from white folks … nothing but God;
8. Abused beyond imagination I was courageous enough to decide for myself that life could be better;
9. Despite being beaten and abused I kept my eyes upon the Father who heard my prayers and saw me though;
10. This can give you encouragement: He heard my cries, my pleas, my prayers and kept me in His hand. Oh, I still went through some stuff (temptations), but it was never more than I could stand underneath, and He has always provided a way out. (I Cor. 10:13)
11. I have been blessed to experience love and His Love throughout my life;

12. This story largely began as I described being laid flat on my back with my chest bandaged up after swallowing poison as a baby, and now even as God is delivering me from cancer, I find myself flat on my back with my chest bandaged up again, getting more good news from my doctors as I heal from their God-directed hands.

I know that my Father in heaven is with me all the time.

ENDING:

As I close this chapter (the end of my autobiography) I pray that it will be published and go on to be a tool that helps someone that doesn't know the miraculous works of my higher power (God and His Son, Jesus Christ), will see that God has even now healed me from breast cancer and I didn't have to take any chemotherapy, and as I finish this spiritual motivational book they will get to know this higher power (God) as I have and His healing powers. I pray that they will want to have a personal relationship with Him and know that He (God) has all of us who believe (has faith) that He will do the same for them in His own way. According to His will for them! Prayerfully, they will know that God has all His believers in His hand and that He has the last word about our lives and how we should live them with Love for one another as He loves us.

I thank God for my wellness journey, and I know for sure that He has had me in His hands every since 1947, May 3rd, when I was born and my mother went to be with Him. Thank you, my heavenly Father. Amen!!

Handwritten completed, 4-1-2021, now on to the typist so that I can get it to the publisher: Author House Publishing. God Bless you, Author House Publishing. I thank all the persons who helped me get it typed and to the publisher. (1) My prayer partner, Verlendia Alexander; (2) Bryan Jones. May God Bless and keep both of you in His hand. I leave you one of my favorite Bible verses from the King James Version of my higher power.

Psalms 91:11: "For he shall give his angels charge over thee, to keep thee in all thy ways."

Little Sarah

My adopted son, Tim Grant and I

Heather and her dad,
Curtis James Stringer, Jr., 2006 - Deceased

Curtis and Sarah, 2000

Heather's other daddy, Keith Williams, husband for 28 years. I chose him after Heather's daddy left us when she was 2 – returned when she was finishing high school.

Derek Perry, 8-28-2000

My brother, Silas, Sr. We are living in
the house he sold me on land contract.

Silas, Sr. was 10 years older than
me. One of my favorites

Me and my friend Ella at Mother Proctor's
house helping her with her flowers

Sarah and Ms. Kirksey,
a teacher at prison

My nephew Corey and wife
Corey deceased at 35 years

Berge – at prison

My daughter and Me. Heather Shantelle
Cobb, now 44 years old and has my only
grandson, Jordon Ronell Jones, now age 13

My favorite warden at the prison,
Little Romeo (Romanowski)

Sarah, teaching Sunday School at St. James MBC
(Before the pandemic of 2019 –
Coronavirus Pandemic 2019

At my desk in MDOC office

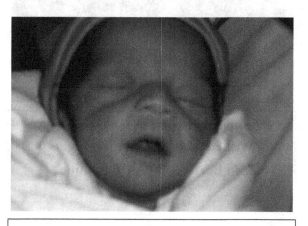

Jordon Jones, grandson at birth, 9-12-2007

Johnnie, old friend; worked at Chrysler
We had fun a many Friday nights
on Bortle #5&6. RIP Johnnie

At the office

Me and two of my volunteers:
Bev Fort and Judge
Bruce Morrow

Heather S. Cobb

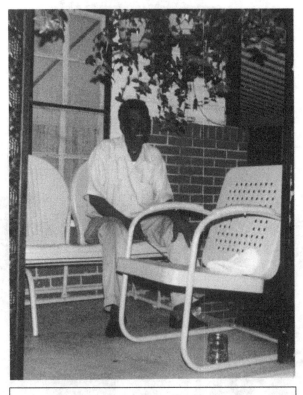

My father, Arthur Lee Cobb, Sr.

Me and Mother Hubbard,
At her apartment for her 102nd Birthday Celebration

Pastor Karl Reid and Marvin Sapp
They both sang with Commissioned
Marvin Sapp has been to our church
and went to dinner with us
lots of times after his wife passed

Jordon at my church, St. James MBC on Kercheval

Church members Verlendia and Mary Nelson

Pastor Karl Reid and wife, Toi Reid
St. James Missionary Baptist Church, 12-23-2018.
10 years of service, 12-8-2018,
40 years of ministry in singing, teaching and counseling

Me and Rusty, St. James MBC at Mother
Hubbard 102nd Birthday celebration. I
cooked dinner for her on Sunday

Mother Hubbard's 102nd Birthday celebration
St. James Missionary Baptist Church

Mother Hubbard's 102nd Birthday Celebration
RIP

RIP Corey Cobb (nephew deceased at age 35) and wife, Kita

At my niece Pam's house

1st Family Reunion
in Miami, Florida
After my father died, 1984

Niece Pam and Me

Heather and her
adopted cousins

Angelique
Cobb, niece

Bev Fort, Little Romeo and Me

Heathie, Me and Curtis

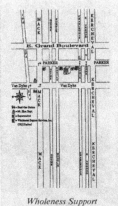

E. Grand Boulevard

Wholeness Support Services, Inc.

Wholeness Support Services, Inc.
(A Non-Profit Corporation)

2922 Parker, Ste. 200
Detroit, Michigan 48214

(313) 304.7029
FAX: (313) 365.5296

Helping you find YOU!

Servicing the Tri-County Area

Sarah M. Cobb, LMSW, ACSW, LSW, CSW – CEO – Wholeness Support Services, Inc.

Sarah M. Cobb has been a practitioner in the field of Family therapy for over twenty (20) years. As CEO of the nonprofit agencies in Michigan providing services to families in all aspects of life issues, we place an emphasis on:

1. Group Therapy
2. Reentry Coaching for Ex-Offenders
3. Substance Abuse Education
4. Crisis Intervention
5. Gerontology Referrals

We also provide 12-Step Programs for Teens and Adults, as well as Mental Health Referrals.

Ms. Cobb is recognized professional as a Special Activity Director for the Michigan Department of corrections at one of the two (2) Detroit-based prisons in Michigan. In her present position she directs and coordinates prisoner-based organizations for over a thousand prisoners. Ms. Cobb also recruits, trains and coordinates over 35 professional volunteers within the prison.

Ms. Cobb is a longtime member of the National Association of Social Workers and an active member of Wayne State University's School of Social Work Alumni Association. She also serves as a Field Instructor for the School of Social Work at Wayne State University.

■ ■ ■

MISSION STATEMENT

To promote a nonviolent and family lifestyle, free from mood altering substances by providing healthy substance abuse prevention education, resources, and motivation to at-risk minority teens and their parents in urban communities of the Detroit Metro Area.

Wholeness Support Services, Inc. wants to help you realize that there are blossoms in each day to be appreciated, and the apparent mountains of life are really a gentle slope when you are prepared to handle them beforehand.

Let us help when there is a need for family therapy in handling unresolved issues of grief, anger, and timely intervention during a crisis. Crisis Intervention scheduling is very flexible as we recognize there will be time when something must be handled immediately. We're here!

We also offer referrals for Gerontology such as Life Lines and support for the home bound, Job Referrals including assessment of skills and individually tailored programming. Ex-offender Therapy will include long-term and short-term assistance with reentry. Recreational Therapy is included.

Individual, Family and Group Sessions are held weekly.

Printed in the United States
by Baker & Taylor Publisher Services